HOW TO PRAY AT ALL TIMES

SAINT ALPHONSUS DE LIGUORI

TRANSLATED BY
A REDEMPTORIST

CATHOLIC WAY
PUBLISHING

Re-typeset and re-published in 2015 by Catholic Way Publishing.
Cover design by Catholic Way Publishing.

This work is published for the greater glory of Jesus Christ through His most holy mother Mary and for the sanctification of the Church militant.

Method of Mental Prayer or Meditation
According to Saint Alphonsus de Liguori.

Translated by T.A.M., C.SS.R. (A Redemptorist),
Mount Saint Alphonsus, Mayfield, N.S.W.

One of the earliest works of Saint Alphonsus first published in 1753. The Saint entitled it: "A method of conversing continually and lovingly with God."

Includes the Stations of the Cross, with 14 Illustrations.

ISBN-13: 978-1-78379-465-2

10 9 8 7 6 5 4 3 2 1

Available in E-Book.

www.catholicwaypublishing.com
London, England, UK
2015

CONTENTS

INTRODUCTION

THIS BEAUTIFUL LITTLE work was first published in 1753. It is therefore one of the earliest works of Saint Alphonsus. The Saint entitled it: "*A method of conversing continually and lovingly with God*"; and to the title, he added a note to say that it had been translated from the French, but that he had "augmented it with holy thoughts, affections and practices." It was surely the Saint's humility that made him thus minimise his part in the composition of the book, for as a matter of fact he entirely recast the little French treatise and made it all his own. His biographer, Father Berthe, could write of it: "In this golden little book are to be found the most familiar thoughts of the holy author." (*Life* Volume I. Page 575).

It will be easily seen that the treatise has a twofold message. Saint Alphonsus, like the Divine Redeemer before him, always puts the thought of God's justice, and the fear of punishment, before those who are obstinate in sin. But, following again the Redeemer's example, the saintly Doctor preaches in burning words the truth that every soul wishing to serve God may go to Him with perfect, unwavering confidence. To such souls, God shows infinite tenderness and love. This message of confidence to men of goodwill, is the first lesson which the Saint teaches, with convincing force, in the following pages. The second lesson is deduced from the first: those who wish to serve God should speak to Him frequently, confidingly, lovingly.

Be it remembered that this treatise is from the pen of a Doctor of the Church: every sentence of it bears the impress of his authority. A new translation of it is now given to the public in the hope that it will continue its mission of mercy, and lead men, in ever increasing numbers, to speak frequently and lovingly to God.

T.A.M., C.SS.R. (A REDEMPTORIST),
MOUNT SAINT ALPHONSUS, MAYFIELD, N.S.W.

HOW TO PRAY AT ALL TIMES

"Watch ye, therefore, praying at all times, that you may be accounted worthy to escape all these things that are to come, and to stand before the Son of Man."
—Saint Luke (21:36).

CHAPTER I

GOD WISHES US TO SPEAK TO HIM WITH CONFIDENCE AND FAMILIARITY

WHAT IS MAN that You should magnify him: or why do You set Your Heart upon him? (Job, 7:17). Such was the astonished cry of Job when he considered the marvellous condescension of God in loving man and in longing to be loved by him. Hence, it is a mistake to think that great confidence and familiarity in treating with God is a want of reverence towards His infinite Majesty. You should, indeed, devout reader, worship Him in all humility and prostrate yourself before Him; especially when you call to mind the ingratitude and sin of which, in the past, you may have been guilty. Yet this should not hinder you from treating Him with the most tender confidence and love. He is infinite majesty; but, at the same time, He is infinite love and goodness. In God you possess the most exalted and supreme Lord; but also a Friend who loves you with the greatest possible love. He is not offended—on the contrary He is pleased—when you treat Him with that confidence, freedom and tenderness with which a child treats its mother. Hear how He invites us to go to Him and even promises to welcome us with His caresses: 'You shall be carried at the breasts and upon the knees they shall caress you. As one whom the mother caresses, so will I comfort you' (Isaiah 66:12). As a mother delights to place her child upon her knees, there to feed or fondle it: so is our merciful God pleased to treat souls whom He loves, who have given themselves wholly to Him, and placed all their hopes in His goodness.

Bear well in mind that you have neither friend, nor brother, nor father, nor mother, nor spouse, nor lover, who loves you more than God. Divine grace is that great treasure whereby we, vile creatures and poor servants, become the dear friends of our Creator Himself: 'For she is an infinite treasure to men, which they that use, become the friends of God (Wisdom 7:14). In order to fill our hearts with confidence, He emptied Himself, as Saint Paul says (Philippians 2:7), abasing Himself to our level and conversing familiarly with us: He conversed with men (Baruch 3:38). He went so far as to become an infant, to become poor, to die publicly on a cross; He went so far as to hide Himself under the appearance of bread in order to become our constant Companion and to unite Himself intimately to us: 'He that eats My Flesh and drinks My Blood abides in Me and I in him (John 6:57). In a word, He loves you as though He had no one else to love but you alone. You, too, should love Him alone, and all others for His sake. Of Him, you may say, and, indeed, you should say: 'My Beloved to me and I to Him' (Canticles 2:16). My God has given Himself all to me, and I give myself all to Him; He has chosen me for His beloved, and I choose Him, of all others, for my only love: 'My Beloved is white and ruddy, chosen out of thousands' (Canticles 5:10).

Say, then, to him, often:

O my Lord! Wherefore do You love me thus? What good thing do You see in me? Have You forgotten the injuries I have done You? But since You have treated me so lovingly, and, instead of casting me into hell, have granted me so many favours, whom can I desire to love from this day forward but You, my God, my all? Ah, most gracious God, if in time past I have offended You, it is not so much the punishment I have deserved that now grieves me, as the displeasure I have given You, who are worthy of infinite love. But You know not how to despise a heart that repents and humbles itself: 'A contrite and humble heart, O God, You will not despise.' (Psalm 51:17 in the Hebrew or Psalm 50:19 in the Vulgate.) Ah, now, indeed, neither in this life nor in the other do I desire any but You alone: 'What have I in heaven? And besides You what do I desire upon earth? You are the God of my heart, and the God that is my portion forever.' (Psalm 73:25–26 in the Hebrew or, in the Vulgate, Psalm 72:25–26) You alone are and shall be forever the only Lord of my heart, of my will; You my only good, my heaven, my hope, my love, my all: "The God of my heart, and the God that is my portion forever."

The more to strengthen your confidence in God, often call to mind His loving treatment of you, and the gracious means He has used to help you to overcome your faults and to detach you from the things of this world, in order to draw you to His holy love. Fear, therefore, to have too little confidence in treating with God, now that you are determined to love Him and to please Him by every means in your power. The mercy which He has shown you is a most sure pledge of His love for you. God is displeased with a want of confidence on the part of souls who sincerely love Him, and whom He loves. If, then, you desire to please His merciful Heart, converse with Him henceforward with the greatest possible confidence and tenderness.

"I have graven you in My hands; your walls are always before My eyes" (Isaiah 49:16). In these words, God says to you in effect: 'Beloved soul, why are you timid or distrustful? I have written you in My hands so as never to forget to do you good. Are you afraid of your enemies? Know that the care of your defence is always before Me, so that I cannot lose sight of it.' This is the thought which made David rejoice, as he cried out to God: 'You have crowned us as with a shield of Your good will.' (Psalm 5:12 in the Hebrew or, in the Vulgate, Psalm 5:13.) Who, Lord, can ever harm us if You do surround us with Your goodness and love?

Let the thought of the gift of our Divine Lord be the greatest motive of your hope: 'God so loved the world as to give His only-begotten Son' (John, 3:16). How can we ever fear, as the Apostle asks, that God would refuse us any good gift, seeing that He has deigned to give us His own Son? He delivered Him up for us all; how has He not also, with Him, given us all things? (Romans 8:32).

'My delights are to be with the children of men' (Proverbs 8:31). If one may so express it—the paradise of God is the heart of man. Does God love you? Love Him in return. His delights are to be with you; let yours be to be with Him—to pass all your lifetime with Him, in whose company you hope to spend a blissful eternity. Accustom yourself to speak to Him alone, familiarly, with confidence and love, as to the dearest friend you have, the Friend who loves you most.

CHAPTER II

IT IS EASY AND AGREEABLE TO CONVERSE WITH GOD

IF, AS HAS been already said, it is a great mistake to speak to God with diffidence—to appear before Him as a timid slave, trembling with alarm before his prince—it would be a still greater mistake to think that conversing with God is wearisome and unpleasant. No—on the contrary her conversation has no bitterness nor her company any tediousness (Wisdom 8:16). Ask those souls who love Him with a true love, and they will tell you that in the sorrows of their life their sweetest and truest consolation is to converse lovingly with God.

Now, you are not required to apply your mind so constantly to prayer as to forget your ordinary work and recreation. "Praying always," means that, without neglecting your ordinary occupations, you treat God as you treat the friends who love you and whom you love. God is ever near you, even within you: 'In Him we live and move and have our being' (Acts 18:28). He who would speak to God has no door to open; God is pleased when you speak to Him without reserve. Tell Him of your business, your plans, your griefs, your fears—of all that concerns you. Above all, do so (as I have already said) with confidence and entire freedom. For

God is not wont to speak to the soul which does not speak to Him; in fact, being unaccustomed to speak to God, the soul would scarcely understand Him when He spoke. This is what the Lord complains of, in these words: 'Our sister is little: what shall we do to our sister in the day when she is to be spoken to?' (Canticles 8:8). Our sister is but a child in My love; what shall we do to speak to her if she understands not? It is the will of God that we remember His surpassing power and His rigorous justice if we despise His grace; but, on the contrary, He wishes that we should treat Him as a most affectionate friend if we love Him, and that we should speak to Him confidingly and without restraint.

It is true that God ought to be worshipped always with the greatest reverence; however, when He deigns to make you feel His presence and when He makes known His desire that you should speak to Him as to the Friend who loves you better than any other friend, then you should open your heart to Him with the greatest liberty and confidence. 'She prevents them that covet her, so that she first shows herself unto them' (Wisdom, 6–16). If you only desire His love, He will take the first step, without waiting for you to come to Him, and He will present Himself to you with all the graces and remedies of which you stand in need. He only waits for you to speak to Him, to show that He is near you, ready to hear and to comfort you: 'And His ears are unto our prayers' (Psalm 34:15 in the Hebrew or, in the Vulgate, Psalm 33:16).

By reason of His immensity, God is present everywhere; but there are two places where He dwells in a particular manner. One is in the highest heavens, where He is present by that glory which He communicates to the blessed; the other is on earth—within the humble soul that loves Him: 'His name is holy who dwells in the high and holy place, and with a contrite and humble spirit (Isaiah 57:15).

(Footnote: Elsewhere Saint Alphonsus has of course written on the third special dwelling of God with men—the sacramental presence of our Lord in the holy Eucharist. In fact, in the earlier editions of the saint's works the present treatise was always published with the *Visits to the Blessed Sacrament.*)

Our God, then, dwells in the heights of heaven, and yet He does not disdain to occupy Himself with His servants day and night in their homes or in their monastic cells. There He bestows on them His divine consolations, the least one of which surpasses all the delights that the world offers, and which He alone does not desire who has never tasted their sweetness: 'Oh, taste and see that the Lord is sweet.' (Psalm 34:8 in the Hebrew or, in the Vulgate, Psalm 33:9).

Friends in the world have generally certain days on which they meet and converse; on other days they are apart; but between God and you, if you wish, there need never be one hour of separation: 'You shall rest, and your sleep shall be sweet: the Lord will be at your side (Proverbs 3:24).

You may sleep, but God will place Himself at your side and watch over you continually: 'I will rest with Him and He will be a comfort in my cares and grief.' (Consult Wisdom 8:9 and 8:16). When you take your rest, He does not leave your bedside. He remains there, always thinking of you, that when you awake in the night He may speak to you by His inspirations, and receive from you in return some act of love, of oblation, of thanksgiving. Thus, He desires to continue even in the hours of the night His sweet and gracious converse with you. Sometimes also, He will speak to you while you sleep, and make you hear His voice, so that in waking you may put in practice what He has spoken: 'I will speak to Him in a dream' (Numbers 12:6).

He is there also in the morning, to hear from you some word of affection, of confidence; to be the depository of your first thoughts, and of all the actions which you promise to perform that day to please Him; of all the griefs, too, which you offer to endure willingly for His glory and love. But as He fails not to present Himself to you at the moment of your waking, do not fail, on your part to give Him immediately a look of love, and to rejoice when your God announces to you the glad tidings that He is not far from you (as once He may have been by reason of your sins); but that He loves you, and would be beloved by you; and at that same moment He gives you the gracious precept, 'You shall love the Lord your God with your whole heart' (Deuteronomy, 6:5).

CHAPTER III

ON WHAT, AND HOW, WE SHOULD CONVERSE WITH GOD

1. IN GENERAL

NEVER, THEN, FORGET His sweet presence, as do the greater part of men. Speak to Him as often as you can, for He does not grow weary of this nor disdain it, as do the lords of the earth. If you love Him, you will not be at a loss what to say to Him. Tell Him all that occurs to you about yourself and your affairs, as you would tell it to a dear friend. Do not look upon Him as a haughty monarch who will converse only with the great and on great matters. He, your God, is pleased to lower Himself to you, and to hear you communicate to Him your smallest and most ordinary concerns. He loves you as much—He has as much care for you—as if He had no one else to think of but you. He is as completely devoted to your interests as though the only end of His providence was to help you, of His almighty power to aid you, of His mercy and goodness to take pity on you, to do you good and to win by His kindness your confidence and love. Manifest to Him, then, freely your whole state of mind and pray to Him to enlighten you that you may perfectly accomplish His holy will. Let all your desires and aims be directed to learn His good pleasure and to do what is agreeable to His divine Heart: 'Commit your way to the Lord'; and 'desire of Him to direct your ways and that all your counsels may abide in Him.' (Psalm 37:5 in the Hebrew or, in the Vulgate, Psalm 36:5 and Tobit 4:20).

Say not: Why disclose all my wants to God, since He already sees and knows them better than I do? Yes, He knows them; but He acts as if He did not know the needs about which you do not speak to Him and for which you do not seek His aid. Our Saviour knew that Lazarus was dead, and yet He acted as if He did not know until Mary (Magdalen) told Him of it; it was then that He comforted her by bringing her brother back to life.

2. PRAY IN YOUR TRIALS

When you are afflicted with sickness, persecution, temptation, or any other trouble, turn at once to God and ask His help. It is enough for you to lay your affliction before Him—to go to Him and say: 'Behold, O Lord, for I am in distress' (Lamentations 1:20). He will not fail to comfort you, or at least to give you strength to suffer the trial with patience, and in this case it will prove a greater good than if He had freed you altogether from it. Tell Him of all the things that make you fear, or make you sad, and say to Him: '*My God, in You are all my hopes*. I offer this cross to You. I resign myself to Your will. Take pity on me and either deliver me from my trial or give me strength to endure it.' He will remember immediately the promise which He made in the Gospel, of consoling and comforting all those who have recourse to Him in tribulation: 'Come to Me all you that labour and are burdened and I will refresh you (Matthew 11:28).

He will not be displeased if you seek comfort from your friends in the hour of trial; but He wishes you to have recourse principally to Him. At least, therefore, when you have had recourse to creatures and they have not been able to console your heart, go to your Creator and say to Him: 'Lord, men have only words; they cannot afford me consolation. I no longer desire to be consoled by them. You alone are my hope; You alone my only love. By You alone do I desire to be comforted and the consolation I ask for, is to do on this occasion what is most pleasing to You. Behold, I am ready to endure this trial for the whole of my life, and for all eternity, if such be Your will. Only help me.'

Do not be afraid of offending Him if you sometimes gently complain, saying: 'Why, Lord, have You retired afar off? (Psalm 10:1 in the Hebrew and in the Vulgate.) 'Lord, You know that I love You, and that I desire nothing but Your love. Have pity on me and help me. Do not abandon me.'

If desolation should continue for a long time and grievously afflict you, unite your voice to the voice of your afflicted Jesus and say: 'My God, my God, why have You forsaken me?' (Matthew 28:46). Let the thought humble you that having offended God, you do not deserve His consolations. At the same time, remember that He permits every thing for your good, and do not lose confidence: 'All things work together unto good to them that love God' (Romans 8:28). Say with courage, even when you feel most troubled and disconsolate: 'The Lord is my light and my salvation; whom shall I fear?' (Psalm 27:1 in the Hebrew or, in the Vulgate, Psalm 26:1). Lord, You will guide me, You will save me; In You do I trust. In You, O Lord, have I hoped; let me never be confounded (Ecclesiasticus 2:11). Reflect that God loves you more than you can love yourself. Why, then, should you be afraid? David brought comfort to his heart saying: 'The Lord is careful for me.' (Psalm 40:17 in the Hebrew or, in the Vulgate, Psalm 39:18). Let such be your sentiments, too, when you pray; and speak in this manner to God: 'Lord, I cast myself into Your arms; and I desire to think only of loving and pleasing You. Behold me ready to do what You ask of me. You do not only will my good, but You are "careful" for it. To You, then, I leave the care of my salvation. In You I rest, and will rest for evermore, since You will that in You I should place all my hopes': 'In peace, in the self-same I will sleep and I will rest; for You, O Lord, singularly have settled me in hope' (Psalm 4:8 in the Hebrew or, in the Vulgate, Psalm 4:9–10)

'Think of the Lord in goodness' (Wisdom 1:1). In these words, the inspired writer exhorts us to have more confidence in the divine mercy than dread of the divine justice. *For God is incomparably more inclined to bestow favours upon us than to chastise us*, as Saint James says: 'Mercy exalts itself above judgment' (2:13). For this reason, Saint Peter exhorts us in all our fears—whether for our temporal or eternal interests—to abandon ourselves entirely to the goodness of God, who has the interests of our salvation at heart: 'Casting all your care upon Him, for He has care of you' (1 Peter 5:7). The royal prophet, David, has the same message of hope when he gives to God the beautiful title of our God and the God who is willing to save us: 'Our God is the God of salvation.' (Psalm 68:20 in the Hebrew or, in the Vulgate, Psalm 67:21). This means, as (Saint Robert) Bellarmine explains it, that it is the will of God, not to condemn, but to save all. He threatens with His displeasure those who despise Him; but He promises mercy to those who fear Him: in the words of the canticle of our Blessed Lady: 'His mercy is from generation to generation to them that fear Him.'

I place before you, devout reader, all these passages from the sacred scriptures, so that if you are ever troubled by the doubt as to whether you will be saved or no—whether you are of the number of the predestined or no—you may take courage at the thought that you know from God's Word that

He desires to save you, if only you are resolved to serve and love Him as He asks of you.

3. PRAY IN YOUR JOYS

When you receive some pleasant news, do not act like some unfaithful and thankless souls who have recourse to God in time of trouble, but forget and forsake Him when things go well with them. Show Him the fidelity that you would show to a sincere friend who rejoices in your happiness. Go at once and tell Him of your joy, and praise Him and give Him thanks, acknowledging your good fortune as a gift from His hands. Rejoice in the fact that you owe your happiness to Him, and place all your joy and comfort in Him: 'I will rejoice in the Lord' (Habakkuk 3:18). 'I have trusted in Your mercy. My heart shall rejoice in Your salvation. (The name "Jesus" means "Saviour" or "Salvation.") I will sing to the Lord, who gives me good things. Yea I will sing to the name of the Lord the most high.' (Psalm 13:6 in the Hebrew or, in the Vulgate, Psalm 12:6) (This Psalm is thus praying: 'I will joy in God my Jesus.' Say to Him: 'My Jesus, I bless, and will ever bless You, for granting me so many favours, when I deserved at Your hands not favours, but chastisements for the affronts I have offered You.' Say to him, with the sacred Spouse: 'All fruits, the new and the old, my Beloved, I have kept for You' (Canticles 7:13). 'Lord, I give You thanks; I keep in memory Your many acts of kindness, past and present, to render You praise and glory for them forever.'

But if you love your God, you ought to rejoice more in His blessedness than in your own. He who has a dear friend sometimes takes more delight in that friend's good fortune than if it had been his own. Comfort yourself, then, in the knowledge that God is infinitely happy. Often say to him: 'My beloved Lord, I rejoice more in Your blessedness than in any happiness of my own, for I love You more than I love myself.'

4. PRAY AFTER A FAULT

Another mark of confidence highly pleasing to our most loving God is this: that when you have committed any fault, you are not ashamed to go at once to Him and seek His pardon. Consider that God is so willing to pardon sinners that He laments their perdition, when they depart far from Him and live dead to His grace. Therefore, does he lovingly call them, saying: 'Why will you die, O house of Israel? Return all of you, and live' (Ezekiel 18:31). He promises to receive a soul that has forsaken Him, if only it returns to His arms: 'Turn to Me . . . and I will turn to you' (Zechariah 1:3). Would that sinners only knew how mercifully our Saviour awaits them in order to pardon them: 'The Lord waits that He may have mercy upon you' (Isaiah 30:18). Would that sinners realised the desire on the part of God, not, indeed, to chastise them, but to see them converted and to embrace and press them to His Heart: 'As I live, says the Lord God, I desire not the death of the wicked, but that the wicked turn from his way and live' (Ezekiel 33:11).

He has even still more consoling words: 'Come and accuse Me, says the Lord; if your sins be as scarlet, they shall be made as white as snow' (Isaiah 1:18). In other words, He says: 'Sinners, repent of having offended Me and then come to Me. If I do not pardon you, accuse Me of being unfaithful to My promises; but, no, I will keep My word. If you come to Me and repent, though your soul be dyed deep crimson with crime, by My grace it shall be made white as snow.' Almighty God promises even to forget the sinner's wrongdoing if only he repents: 'I will not remember all his iniquities' (Ezekiel 18:22). As soon, then, as you fall into any fault, raise your eyes to God, make an act of love, and humbly confessing your fault, place unwavering confidence in God, saying to Him: 'Lord, behold, he whom You love is sick' (John 11:3). The heart which You love is sick—is wounded. 'Heal my soul, for I have sinned against You.' (Psalm 41:4 in the Hebrew or, in the Vulgate, Psalm 40:5). 'You seek penitent sinners. Behold one at Your feet, seeking You. The evil is committed—what must I do? You will not have me lose confidence; even after the sin which I have committed, You desire my good, and I again love You. Yes, my God I love You with all my heart. I am sorry for my sin, and will never more offend You.' 'You are a God, sweet, and mild, and plenteous in mercy.' (Psalm 86:5 in the Hebrew or, in the Vulgate, Psalm 85:5.) 'Pardon me. Let me hear from You what You did say to Magdalen: "Your sins are forgiven you" (Luke 7:48); and give me strength for the future to be faithful to You.'

Then, in order not to be discouraged, cast your eyes upon Jesus Christ crucified; offer to the Eternal Father his merits, and confidently hope for pardon; since to pardon you he spared not his own Son. Say to him with confidence: 'Look on the face of Your Christ–Your Anointed One.' (Psalm 84:9 in the Hebrew or, in the Vulgate, Psalm 83:10.) 'My God, have regard to Your Son who has died for me and for His sake grant me pardon.'

Attend, especially, devout soul, to what is commonly taught by masters of the spiritual life, who recommend you to have recourse immediately to God after you have fallen, although you should repeat the fall a hundred times in the day. Having done this, do not be disturbed. If you remain discouraged and troubled because of the fault committed, you will scarcely speak to God; your confidence will grow less your desire to love God will grow cold and you will make little or no advance in the way of the Lord. On the other hand, by having immediate recourse to God, asking His pardon and promising amendment for the future, your very faults will help you to advance in divine love. Between friends who sincerely love one another, it sometimes happens that when one offends the other and then humbles himself and asks pardon, their friendship becomes stronger than ever. Do you act in like manner with regard to God: let your faults only strengthen the bonds of love, which unite you to Him.

5. PRAY IN YOUR DOUBTS

Whenever you are in doubt about anything—whether it regards yourself or others—act like good friends do, who always consult one another in their difficulties. Show the same mark of confidence to God; consult Him; ask Him to enlighten you, that you may decide on what is most pleasing to Him: 'Put You words in my mouth and strengthen the resolution in my heart' (Judith 9:18). Lord, make known to me what You would have me do, to answer, and I will obey You: 'Speak, Lord, for Your servant hears (1 Samuel 3:10 in the Hebrew or, in the Vulgate, 1 Kings 3:10).

6. PRAY FOR YOUR NEIGHBOUR

Recommend to God with confidence not only your own needs but also the needs of others. How pleasing to Him it will be if you sometimes forget yourself and speak to Him of His own glory, of the miseries of others, especially those who mourn in sorrow; of the souls in purgatory, His spouses, who long to behold Him in Heaven; and of poor sinners who live deprived of His grace. Pray to Him for sinners thus:

Lord, You are all goodness and worthy of an infinite love: how, then, can You endure in the world so many souls on whom You have lavished Your favours, and who yet have no desire to know You, who have no desire to love You, who even offend and despise You? Ah, my most amiable God, make Yourself known—make Yourself loved. 'Hallowed be Your name.' 'Your kingdom come.' May Your name be adored and loved by all men. May Your love reign in all hearts. Do not let me depart from You without granting me some grace for the unhappy souls for whom I pray.

7. SPEAK TO GOD OF HEAVEN

It is said that souls who in this life have but little longing for heaven are punished in purgatory with a peculiar pain, called the pain of languor. This surely is only just; because to have but little longing for heaven is to set little value on the happiness of that eternal kingdom which our Lord opened to us by His death. Remember, then, frequently to think of, and long for heaven. Say to God that your life seems an endless span, so great is your desire to go to Him, to see Him face to face, and to love Him. Long to be set free from your exile, from this world of sin, from the danger of losing divine grace, that you may arrive at that land of love where your heart will be given wholly to God. Say to Him over and over again: 'Lord, as long as I live on this earth I am in danger of forsaking You and of losing Your love. When shall I leave this life, wherein I am forever offending You? When shall I go to love You with all my soul and unite myself to You without any danger of losing You again?'

Saint Teresa was ever sighing for heaven in this manner. She used to rejoice when she heard the clock strike, because another hour of life and of the danger of losing God, had passed. She so earnestly desired to die that she might see God, that she was dying with the desire to die. This was the subject of the loving poem which she composed: "I die because I do not die."

CHAPTER IV

HOW GOD ANSWERS THE SOUL

IN A WORD, if you wish to please the loving Heart of God, endeavour to speak to Him as often as you can, and with the fullest confidence that He will answer and speak to you in return. When you withdraw yourself from conversation with creatures to speak to God alone, He will not speak in a voice that strikes the ear, but in a voice that reaches the heart: 'I will lead her into the wilderness and I will speak to her heart' (Hosea or Osee, 2:14). He will speak by inspiration, by interior light, by manifestations of His goodness, by a tenderness which touches the heart, by assurance of pardon, by a feeling of peace, by the hope of heaven, by intimate happiness, by the sweetness of His grace, by loving and tender embraces of the soul—in a word, He will speak in a voice easily understood by those whom He loves and who have given their hearts to Him.

CHAPTER V

THE PRACTICE OF PRAYING CONSTANTLY

TO CONCLUDE THIS treatise, I will recall briefly, what has been said in the preceding pages, and I will suggest a practice by which you may render all your daily actions pleasing to God.

When you awake in the morning, let your first thought be to raise up your mind to God, to offer to His honour whatever you may have to do or suffer during the day, and to beseech Him to assist you with His holy grace. Then perform your other morning devotions, making acts of love and of gratitude, and praying and resolving to spend the day as if it were to be the last of your life.

Father Saint-Jure recommends you to make a compact every morning with God, that every time you make a certain sign, such as placing your hand upon your heart, or raising your eyes to heaven or to the crucifix, or the like, you intend thereby to make an act of love, of desire to see God loved by all, of oblation of yourself, and other acts of the same kind. When you have made these acts, place your soul in the wound of the side of Jesus and under the mantle of Mary, and beg of the Eternal Father, for the love of Jesus and Mary, to protect you during the day. Then, before all things else, be sure to make your meditation, or mental prayer, at least for half an hour. Meditate especially on the sufferings and contempt which Jesus endured in His Passion. This is the subject dearest to fervent souls, and the one best calculated to set hearts aflame with divine love. If you desire to make progress in the spiritual life, there are three devotions which must be particularly dear to you: Devotion to the Passion of our Lord, to the Most Blessed Sacrament and to the Blessed Virgin Mary.

In all your meditations repeat again and again acts of contrition, of the love of God and of oblation of yourself. The venerable Father Charles Caraffa, (1561–1633) founder of the Congregation of Pious Workers, says that one fervent act of love made thus in the morning is sufficient to maintain the soul in fervour throughout the whole day.

Perform your more important acts of devotion with great care, such as going to confession, receiving Holy Communion, reciting the divine office, and other similar duties. Whenever you are going to begin some external occupation, like study or work, or the duty of your state in life, do not forget to offer it to God, praying His assistance to enable you to perform it well. Afterwards follow the example of Saint Catharine of Siena and retire often to the cell of your heart in order to unite yourself to God. In a word, whatever you do, do it with God and for Him. When you leave your room, or go out of the house—and when you return—say a Hail Mary, and thus recommend yourself to the Blessed Virgin. At your meals, whether you find them pleasant to your taste, or not to your liking, offer all to God. On rising from table, say, as grace, some little prayer like this: 'Lord, how good You are to one who has offended You!' During the day give some time to spiritual reading; and make a visit to the Blessed Sacrament and to our Lady. In the evening say the Rosary, examine your conscience, make acts of faith, hope, charity and contrition; promise to serve God more fervently and to receive the holy sacraments during life and at death, and form the intention of gaining all the indulgences within your power. When you go to bed, reflect that you have deserved to lie in the fire of hell; then, with a crucifix in your arms, compose yourself to sleep, saying: 'In peace, in the self-same I will sleep and I will rest.' (Psalm 4:8 in the Hebrew or, in the Vulgate, Psalm 4:9.)

(Here, in passing, {Saint Alphonsus adds,} I would remind the reader of indulgences which are attached to various acts of devotion; and also I would remind him of the desirability of renewing each morning the intention of gaining all the indulgences possible during the day. For reciting the acts of faith, hope and charity there is an indulgence of seven years and seven quarantines each day. {A Quarantine is the remission of as much temporal punishment as would be blotted out by an ecclesial penance of forty days.} If they are recited daily for a month, a plenary indulgence may be gained on the condition of going to confession and Communion and of praying for the intentions of the Church; this indulgence may be applied to the souls in purgatory or to oneself at the hour of death.) [Since the revisions of Vatican II, all indulgences are now classed either as 'partial' or as 'plenary.' Let us recall, however, that God is never outdone in generosity.]

(In like manner, form the intention of gaining also all the indulgences granted for saying the Rosary on beads properly blessed, the Angelus three times a day, the Litany of our Blessed Lady, the 'Salve Regina' {Hail Holy Queen}, the 'Ave Maria' {Hail Mary}, and the 'Gloria Patri' {Glory be to the Father}; for saying, "Blessed be the holy and Immaculate Conception of the most Blessed Virgin Mary, Mother of God"; as also for saying, "Blessed and praised every moment be the most holy and divine Sacrament"; for reciting the prayer 'Anima Christi' {Soul of Christ or 'Soul of my Saviour'—the hymn}, et cetera; for bowing the head at the 'Gloria Patri' and at the most holy names of Jesus and Mary; as also for hearing Mass; for making half an hour's mental prayer—for this there is a partial indulgence, and also, if the meditation is made daily, a plenary indulgence on the usual conditions of confession, Communion and praying for the intentions of the Church; for genuflecting before the Blessed Sacrament; for kissing the cross.)

{Footnote from the 1957 Redemptorist editor regarding genuflecting before the Blessed Sacrament: The recent edition of the *Raccolta*, (the book formally listing indulgenced prayers) No. 116a, quotes this indulgence in these terms: "Any exterior act of reverence when passing a Church or Chapel where the Blessed Sacrament is reserved," 100 days 'Toties Quoties' ('as often as it is done'). For kissing the cross, the new *Raccolta* gives no indulgence.}

In order to keep yourself recollected and united to God as far as the imperfections of human nature permit, endeavour, by means of what you see and hear, *to raise your mind to God and to recall the things of eternity*. For instance, when you see running water, reflect that your life is rushing on in like manner and taking you nearer to death. When you see a lamp going out for want of oil, reflect that thus your life will one day flicker out and be extinguished. When you see graves or the bodies of the dead, think of what will happen to yourself one day. When you see worldly people rejoicing in their wealth or distinction, have pity on their folly, and say to yourself: 'For me God is sufficient': 'Some trust in chariots, some in horses, but we in the name of the Lord' (Psalm 20:7 in the Hebrew or, in the Vulgate, Psalm 19:8). 'Let them glory if they wish in vanity. Be it mine to glory only in the grace of God and in His holy love.' When you see monuments erected to the dead, or take part in the funeral ceremonies of the great ones of this world, ask yourself the question: 'If their souls are lost, what will all this pomp avail them?' When you look out over the ocean and see it now calm and tranquil and now lashed to fury by the winds, consider the difference there is between a soul in sin and a soul in the state of grace. When you see a tree that is withered, reflect on the fact that a soul without God is fit for nothing but to be cast into the fire.

If you ever happen to see one who has been guilty of some great crime, trembling with shame and fear in the presence of his judge, or his father, or of his Bishop, consider what the terror of the sinner will be in the presence of Jesus Christ, his judge. When thunder crashes through the heavens, and you grow alarmed, reflect how those miserable souls that are damned tremble as they hear continually in hell the thunders of the divine wrath. If you ever see one who has been condemned to suffer a painful death, and who says, "Is there, then, no longer any means of my escaping death?" consider what will be the despair of a soul when it is condemned to hell, as it says: "Is there, then, no longer any means of escaping from eternal ruin?"

When you behold beautiful scenes in the country or along the sea coast, or when you look at flowers or fruit, and are pleased by the sight or the perfume, say: '*For me God has created these lovely things in this world, that I may love Him.* What delights has He not prepared for me in heaven?' Seeing fair plains and beautiful hills, Saint Teresa used to say that they reproached her with her ingratitude to God. The Abbot de Rance, founder of La Trappe, declared that the beauty of creation around him obliged him to love God. Saint Augustine had the same thought: "The heavens and the earth and all Your works cry out to me to love You." There is a story told of a certain holy man, that in passing through the fields he would strike with a little stick the flowers and plants which he found on his way, saying, "Be silent; do not reproach me any longer for my ingratitude to God. I have understood you; be silent; say no more." When Saint Mary Magdalene of Pazzi held in her hand any beautiful fruit or flower, she used to feel herself glowing with divine love, saying to herself, "Behold, my God has thought from eternity of creating this fruit, this flower, in order to give it to me as a token of the love which He bears towards me."

When you see rivers or streams, reflect that as their waters run towards the sea, and never remain still, *so ought you ever tend towards God, who is your only good.* When you happen to be in some vehicle drawn by horses say: "See what labour these innocent animals go through for my service; and how much pains do I myself take in order to serve and please my God?" When you see a little dog, which for a miserable morsel of bread is faithful to its master, reflect how much greater reason you have to be faithful to God, who has created and preserved you, and heaps upon you so many blessings. When you hear the birds sing, say: "Hearken, O my soul, to the praise which these little creatures are giving to their Creator; and what are you doing?" Then do you also praise him with acts of love. On the other hand, when you hear the cock crow, recall to your memory that there once was a time when you also, like Peter, denied your God; and renew your tears and your contrition. If you see the house or the locality in which you fell into some sin, turn to God and say in your heart: 'The sins of my youth and my ignorance; remember not, O Lord.' (Psalm 25:7 in the Hebrew or, in the Vulgate, Psalm 24:7).

When you see valleys fertilised by waters that descend on them from the heights of the mountains, consider that grace in a similar manner leaves those who are proud, to flow into hearts that are humble. When you see a church beautifully adorned, consider the beauty of a soul in grace, which is truly the temple of God. When you look upon the sea, consider the greatness and immensity of God. When you see fire, or candles lighted on the altar say: "For how many years ought I to have been burning in hell? But since You, O Lord, have not yet condemned me to that place of woe, grant that my heart may now burn with Your holy love, even as this fuel or these candles." When you behold the heavens and the stars, say with Saint Andrew of Avellino (1521–1608): "My feet will one day tread upon those stars."

Recall also frequently the mysteries of our Saviour's love; and when you see straw or a manger or a rocky cave, remember the Infant Jesus and the stable at Bethlehem. When, you see a hammer, or a saw, or a plane, or an axe, recall how Jesus laboured like any ordinary young working man in the cottage at Nazareth. If you see cords, thorns, nails, or beams of wood, think of the sorrows and death of the Most Holy Redeemer. When Saint Francis of Assisi happened to see a lamb, he shed tears, as he exclaimed: "My Lord like a lamb was led to die for me." When you look at an altar, a chalice, or a chasuble, recall to mind the great love which Jesus has shown us in giving Himself to us in the Sacrament of the Holy Eucharist.

Following the example of Saint Teresa, often offer yourself to God during the day, and say: "Behold me, O Lord, ready to do what You will. Make known to me Your holy will; I am eager to do all that You ask of me."

As the hours go by, make repeated acts of divine love, for—to quote Saint Teresa again—these acts of love are the fuel by which divine love is kept burning within the heart. One day, when the Venerable Sister Seraphine of Capri (Serafina di Dio, 1621–1699) happened to see the convent mule, the thought occurred to her that the poor animal could not love God. She expressed her compassion in these words: "Poor brute you can neither know nor love God." Then a wonderful thing happened—tears welled into the animal's eyes and forthwith began to flow abundantly. Do you imitate the saintly sister's example. When you see, creatures incapable of knowing or loving God, use the intelligence that He has given you to repeat many acts of love.

If anything painful or disagreeable happens to you, immediately offer to God what you have to suffer, and unite your will to His. Accustom yourself to repeat in every trial: 'It is the will of God; it is my will also.' Acts of resignation are the acts of love dearest to the Heart of God.

When you have to arrive at some decision, or to give some important advice, ask God's help before you do so. Repeat as often as you reasonably can during the day: 'Incline unto mine aid, O God,' as Saint Rose of Lima was accustomed to do. To obtain this help of God turn frequently to the crucifix or to the picture of our Blessed Lady (which, of course, you will have in your room) and do not fail to invoke frequently the names of Jesus and Mary, especially in time of temptation. God, being infinitely kind, has the greatest desire to communicate His graces to us. The Venerable Father Alphonsus Alvarez saw our Lord, on one occasion, with His hands filled with graces, going about seeking souls to whom He might dispense them. But He will have us ask Him for them: Ask and you shall receive; otherwise, He will withdraw His hands. He will, on the contrary, stretch them out to us and willingly open them to us if we invoke Him. Who ever had recourse to God, asks Ecclesiasticus, and God despised him by refusing to hear him? 'Who has called upon Him, and He despised him?' (2–11). David declares that God shows not only mercy, but great mercy, to those who invoke Him: 'For You, O Lord, are sweet and mild; and plenteous in mercy to all that call upon You.' (Psalm 86:5 in the Hebrew or, in the Vulgate, Psalm 85:5).

How good and kind God is to those who lovingly seek Him! 'The Lord is good to the soul that seeks Him' (Lamentations 3:25). He is found even by those who do not seek Him: 'I was found by them that did not seek Me' (Romans 10:20); with far greater willingness He will anticipate those who seek Him in order to serve and love Him.

I conclude with a thought from Saint Teresa. It is this: 'The souls of the just should do on earth, through a spirit of love, what the Blessed do in heaven. In heaven, the saints occupy themselves only with God; all their thoughts are for His glory; all their pleasure is to love Him. Do you act in the same way. During your life on earth let God be your only happiness, the only object of your affections, the only end of all your actions and desires, until you arrive at that eternal Kingdom, where your love will be consummated and made perfect, and your desires will be completely fulfilled and satisfied.'

APPENDIX

METHOD OF MENTAL PRAYER or Meditation According to Saint Alphonsus.

I. PREPARATION

A recollected life and regular Spiritual Reading are the best remote preparation.

For the immediate preparation, make three short but fervent acts.

(1) An Act of Adoration of God present to the soul.

Example: 'O my God, I believe You are really here present; I bow down and adore You. You are so good, I am so sinful; You are so great, I am only nothingness'; et cetera.

(2) An Act of Sorrow for Sin.

Example: 'O my God, I am heartily sorry for all my sins of thought, word, deed, and omission, and by the help of Your holy grace I will never sin again.'

(3) A Petition for Light and Strength.

Example: 'O my God, give me light to see Your holy Will, give me grace to do Your Will. *O Wisdom of the Sacred Heart of Jesus, direct me in all my ways.* O Love of the Sacred Heart, consume me in Your fire.

Add a Hail Mary to the Blessed Virgin and an ejaculation to Saint Joseph, your Patron Saints and Angel Guardian.

II. BODY OF THE PRAYER

Use the mind in thinking on some subject as much as is necessary in order to pray fervently. But do not imagine that very much is necessary in order to pray. Do not wait for a great fire to burn up in your soul, but cherish any little spark you may feel.

To help your mind, read a text of Scripture or a short Meditation out of a book. Saint Teresa used a book in her Meditations for seventeen years.

Meditate for a few minutes on any thought that has struck you; that is, think for a short time on what it means, what lessons it teaches you, and ask yourself: 'What have I done about this hitherto? What shall I now do?' But remember, you think only in order that you may pray.

The great benefit of Mental Prayer consists less in meditation or thinking than in acts, prayers and resolutions, which are the fruits of Meditation. The thinking is the needle which draws after it the golden thread of acts, prayers and resolutions. The thread is more important than the needle. The chief part of the time of Meditation should, then, be spent in making:

1. ACTS AND AFFECTIONS

Examples.—Acts of Humility: "My God, I am nothing in Your sight."

Act of Thanksgiving: "My God, I thank You for Your goodness."

Act of Love: "My God, I love You with my whole heart. I wish to please You in all things. I will only what You will. I love You because You are infinitely good. Do with me and mine all that pleases You, because it is Your will."

Acts of love and of contrition are golden chains binding us to God. Saint Thomas says: "Every act of love merits eternal life." Make then many simple but fervent acts of love and sorrow.

2. PRAYERS OF PETITION

In mental prayer, it is extremely useful, and, perhaps better than all else, to make many earnest petitions for the graces you want.

Always ask, above all, for

(a) the perfect forgiveness of all past sin;

(b) the perfect love of God; and

(c) the grace of a holy death.

"At first," said Father Paul Segneri, S.J., "I used to employ my time of prayer in reflections and affections, but God opened my eyes, and then I gave myself to petitions, and if I have any good, it comes from this practice."

3. RESOLUTIONS

"The progress of a soul," says Saint Teresa, "does not consist in thinking much of God, but in loving Him, and this love is gained by resolving to do much for Him." Make one practical resolution that you mean to keep during the day.

III. CONCLUSION

Three short fervent acts:

(1) Thank God for the light He has given you.

(2) Renew your resolution to abstain from some fault or to do some good thing, during the day.

(3) Ask the Eternal Father, for the love of Jesus and Mary, to help you to keep it.

At the end of meditation, always pray for poor sinners and for the souls in Purgatory.

N.B.—The acts and prayers of petition should occupy the most of the time. Thus, in a half-hour's prayer, give three minutes to the preparation: think for five minutes and then pray.

THE WAY OF THE CROSS

KNEELING before the altar, make an Act of Contrition, and form the intention of gaining the indulgences, whether for yourself or for the souls in Purgatory.

PREPARATORY PRAYER

My Lord Jesus Christ, Thou hast made this journey to die for me with love unutterable, and I have so many times unworthily abandoned Thee; but now I love Thee with my whole heart, and because I love Thee, I repent sincerely for ever having offended Thee. Pardon me, my God, and permit me to accompany Thee on this journey. Thou goest to die for love of me; I wish also, my beloved Redeemer, to die for love of Thee. My Jesus, I will live and die always united to Thee.

STATION 1: JESUS IS CONDEMNED TO DEATH

STATION 1

Jesus is Condemned to Death

V. We adore Thee, O Christ, and we bless Thee.

R. Because by Thy holy Cross, Thou hast redeemed the world.

Consider how Jesus, after having been scourged and crowned with thorns, was unjustly condemned by Pilate to die on the Cross.

My adorable Jesus, it was not Pilate, no, it was my sins that condemned Thee to die. I beseech Thee, by the merits of this sorrowful journey, to assist my soul in its journey towards eternity. I love Thee, my beloved Jesus; I repent with my whole heart for having offended Thee. Never permit me to separate myself from Thee again. Grant that I may love Thee always; and then do with me what Thou wilt.

Our Father, Hail Mary and Glory Be.

Dear Jesus, Thou dost go to die
For very love of me:
Ah! let me bear Thee company;
I wish to die with Thee.

V. Have mercy on us, O Lord.

R. Have mercy on us.

STATION 2: JESUS BEARS HIS CROSS

STATION 2

Jesus Bears His Cross

V. We adore Thee, O Christ, and we bless Thee.

R. Because by Thy holy Cross, Thou hast redeemed the world.

Consider how Jesus, in making this journey with the Cross on His shoulders thought of us, and for us offered to His Father the death He was about to undergo.

My most beloved Jesus, I embrace all the tribulations Thou hast destined for me until death. I beseech Thee, by the merits of the pain Thou didst suffer in carrying Thy Cross, to give me the necessary help to carry mine with perfect patience and resignation. I love Thee, Jesus my love; I repent of having offended Thee. Never permit me to separate myself from Thee again. Grant that I may love Thee always; and then do with me what Thou wilt.

Our Father, Hail Mary and Glory Be.

Dear Jesus, Thou dost go to die
For very love of me:
Ah! let me bear Thee company;
I wish to die with Thee.

V. Have mercy on us, O Lord.

R. Have mercy on us.

STATION 3: JESUS FALLS THE FIRST TIME

STATION 3

Jesus Falls the First Time

V. We adore Thee, O Christ, and we bless Thee.

R. Because by Thy holy Cross, Thou hast redeemed the world.

Consider this first fall of Jesus under His Cross. His flesh was torn by the scourges, His head crowned with thorns, and He had lost a great quantity of blood. He was so weakened that he could scarcely walk, and yet he had to carry this great load upon His shoulders. The soldiers struck Him rudely, and thus He fell several times in His journey.

My beloved Jesus, it is not the weight of the Cross, but my sins, which have made Thee suffer so much pain. Ah, by the merits of this first fall, deliver me from the misfortune of falling into mortal sin. I love Thee, O my Jesus, with my whole heart; I repent of having offended Thee. Never permit me to separate myself from Thee again. Grant that I may love Thee always; and then do with me what Thou wilt.

Our Father, Hail Mary and Glory Be.

Dear Jesus, Thou dost go to die
For very love of me:
Ah! let me bear Thee company;
I wish to die with Thee.

V. Have mercy on us, O Lord.

R. Have mercy on us.

STATION 4: JESUS MEETS HIS MOTHER

STATION 4

JESUS MEETS HIS MOTHER

V. We adore Thee, O Christ, and we bless Thee.

R. Because by Thy holy Cross, Thou hast redeemed the world.

Consider the meeting of the Son and the Mother, which took place on this journey. Jesus and Mary looked at each other, and their looks became as so many arrows to wound those hearts which loved each other so tenderly.

My most loving Jesus, by the sorrow Thou didst experience in this meeting, grant me the grace of a truly devoted love for Thy most holy Mother. And thou, my Queen, who wast overwhelmed with sorrow, obtain for me by thy intercession a continual and tender remembrance of the Passion of thy Son. I love Thee, Jesus my love; I repent of ever having offended Thee. Never permit me to offend Thee again. Grant that I may love Thee always; and then do with me what Thou wilt.

Our Father, Hail Mary and Glory Be.

Dear Jesus, Thou dost go to die
For very love of me:
Ah! let me bear Thee company;
I wish to die with Thee.

V. Have mercy on us, O Lord.

R. Have mercy on us.

STATION 5: JESUS IS HELPED BY SIMON

STATION 5

JESUS IS HELPED BY SIMON

V. We adore Thee, O Christ, and we bless Thee.

R. Because by Thy holy Cross, Thou hast redeemed the world.

Consider how the Jews, seeing that at each step Jesus from weakness was on the point of expiring, and fearing that He would die on the way, when they wished Him to die the ignominious death of the Cross, constrained Simon the Cyrenian to carry the Cross behind our Lord.

My most sweet Jesus, I will not refuse the Cross, as the Cyrenian did; I accept it; I embrace it. I accept in particular the death Thou hast destined for me; with all the pains that may accompany it; I unite it to Thy death, I offer it to Thee. Thou hast died for love of me; I will die for love of Thee, and to please Thee. Help me by Thy grace. I love Thee, Jesus my love; I repent of having offended Thee. Never permit me to offend Thee again. Grant that I may love Thee always; and then do with me what Thou wilt.

Our Father, Hail Mary and Glory Be.

Dear Jesus, Thou dost go to die
For very love of me:
Ah! let me bear Thee company;
I wish to die with Thee.

V. Have mercy on us, O Lord.

R. Have mercy on us.

STATION 6: VERONICA WIPES THE FACE OF JESUS

STATION 6

VERONICA WIPES THE FACE OF JESUS

V. We adore Thee, O Christ, and we bless Thee.

R. Because by Thy holy Cross, Thou hast redeemed the world.

Consider how the holy woman named Veronica, seeing Jesus so afflicted, and His face bathed in sweat and blood, presented Him with a towel, with which He wiped His adorable face, leaving on it the impression of His holy countenance.

My most beloved Jesus, Thy face was beautiful before, but in this journey it has lost all its beauty, and wounds and blood have disfigured it. Alas, my soul also was once beautiful, when it received Thy grace in Baptism; but I have disfigured it since by my sins; Thou alone, my Redeemer, canst restore it to its former beauty. Do this by Thy Passion, O Jesus. I repent of having offended Thee. Never permit me to offend Thee again. Grant that I may love Thee always; and then do with me what Thou wilt.

Our Father, Hail Mary and Glory Be.

Dear Jesus, Thou dost go to die
For very love of me:
Ah! let me bear Thee company;
I wish to die with Thee.

V. Have mercy on us, O Lord.

R. Have mercy on us.

STATION 7: JESUS FALLS A SECOND TIME

STATION 7

Jesus Falls a Second Time

V. We adore Thee, O Christ, and we bless Thee.

R. Because by Thy holy Cross, Thou hast redeemed the world.

Consider the second fall of Jesus under the Cross—a fall which renews the pain of all the wounds of the head and members of our afflicted Lord.

My most gentle Jesus, how many times Thou hast pardoned me, and how many times have I fallen again, and begun again to offend Thee! Oh, by the merits of this new fall, give me the necessary help to persevere in Thy grace until death. Grant that in all temptations which assail me I may always commend myself to Thee. I love Thee, Jesus my love; I repent of having offended Thee. Never permit me to offend Thee again. Grant that I may love Thee always; and then do with me what Thou wilt.

Our Father, Hail Mary and Glory Be.

Dear Jesus, Thou dost go to die
For very love of me:
Ah! let me bear Thee company;
I wish to die with Thee.

V. Have mercy on us, O Lord.

R. Have mercy on us.

STATION 8: JESUS SPEAKS TO THE WOMEN

STATION 8

JESUS SPEAKS TO THE WOMEN

V. We adore Thee, O Christ, and we bless Thee.

R. Because by Thy holy Cross, Thou hast redeemed the world.

Consider how those women wept with compassion at seeing Jesus in such a pitiable state, streaming with blood, as He walked along. But Jesus said to them: Weep not for Me, but for your children.

My Jesus, laden with sorrows, I weep for the offences I have committed against Thee, because of the pains they have deserved, and still more because of the displeasure they have caused Thee, who hast loved me so much. It is Thy love, more than the fear of hell, which causes me to weep for my sins. My Jesus, I love Thee more than myself; I repent of having offended Thee. Never permit me to offend Thee again. Grant that I may love Thee always; and then do with me what Thou wilt.

Our Father, Hail Mary and Glory Be.

Dear Jesus, Thou dost go to die
For very love of me:
Ah! let me bear Thee company;
I wish to die with Thee.

V. Have mercy on us, O Lord.

R. Have mercy on us.

STATION 9: JESUS FALLS A THIRD TIME

STATION 9

JESUS FALLS A THIRD TIME

V. We adore Thee, O Christ, and we bless Thee.

R. Because by Thy holy Cross, Thou hast redeemed the world.

Consider the third fall of Jesus Christ. His weakness was extreme, and the cruelty of His executioners was excessive, who tried to hasten His steps when He had scarcely strength to move.

Ah, my outraged Jesus, by the merits of the weakness Thou didst suffer in going to Calvary, give me strength sufficient to conquer all human respect, and all my wicked passions, which have led me to despise Thy friendship. I love Thee, Jesus my love, with my whole heart; I repent of having offended Thee. Never permit me to offend Thee again. Grant that I may love Thee always; and then do with me what Thou wilt.

Our Father, Hail Mary and Glory Be.

Dear Jesus, Thou dost go to die
For very love of me:
Ah! let me bear Thee company;
I wish to die with Thee.

V. Have mercy on us, O Lord.

R. Have mercy on us.

STATION 10: JESUS IS STRIPPED OF HIS GARMENTS

STATION 10

JESUS IS STRIPPED OF HIS GARMENTS

V. We adore Thee, O Christ, and we bless Thee.

R. Because by Thy holy Cross, Thou hast redeemed the world.

Consider the violence with which the executioners stripped Jesus. His inner garments adhered to His torn flesh, and they dragged them off so roughly that the skin came with them. Compassionate your Savior thus cruelly treated, and say to Him:

My innocent Jesus, by the merits of the torment Thou hast felt, help me to strip myself of all affection to things of earth, in order that I may place all my love in Thee, who art so worthy of my love. I love Thee, O Jesus, with my whole heart; I repent of having offended Thee. Never permit me to offend Thee again. Grant that I may love Thee always; and then do with me what Thou wilt.

Our Father, Hail Mary and Glory Be.

Dear Jesus, Thou dost go to die
For very love of me:
Ah! let me bear Thee company;
I wish to die with Thee.

V. Have mercy on us, O Lord.

R. Have mercy on us.

STATION 11: JESUS IS NAILED TO THE CROSS

STATION 11

Jesus is Nailed to the Cross

V. We adore Thee, O Christ, and we bless Thee.

R. Because by Thy holy Cross, Thou hast redeemed the world.

Consider how Jesus, after being thrown on the Cross extended His hands, and offered to His Eternal Father the sacrifice of His death for our salvation. These barbarians fastened Him with nails, and then, raising the Cross, allowed Him to die with anguish on this infamous gibbet.

My Jesus! loaded with contempt, nail my heart to Thy feet, that it may ever remain there, to love Thee, and never quit Thee again. I love Thee more than myself; I repent of having offended Thee. Never permit me to offend Thee again. Grant that I may love Thee always; and then do with me what Thou wilt.

Our Father, Hail Mary and Glory Be.

Dear Jesus, Thou dost go to die
For very love of me:
Ah! let me bear Thee company;
I wish to die with Thee.

V. Have mercy on us, O Lord.

R. Have mercy on us.

STATION 12: JESUS DIES ON THE CROSS

STATION 12

Jesus Dies on the Cross

V. We adore Thee, O Christ, and we bless Thee.

R. Because by Thy holy Cross, Thou hast redeemed the world.

Consider how thy Jesus, after three hours' Agony on the Cross, consumed at length with anguish, abandons Himself to the weight of His body, bows His head, and dies.

O my dying Jesus, I kiss devoutly the Cross on which Thou didst die for love of me. I have merited by my sins to die a miserable death; but Thy death is my hope. Ah, by the merits of Thy death, give me grace to die, embracing Thy feet, and burning with love for Thee. I yield my soul into Thy hands. I love Thee with my whole heart; I repent of ever having offended Thee. Never permit me to offend Thee again. Grant that I may love Thee always; and then do with me what Thou wilt.

Our Father, Hail Mary and Glory Be.

Dear Jesus, Thou dost go to die
For very love of me:
Ah! let me bear Thee company;
I wish to die with Thee.

V. Have mercy on us, O Lord.

R. Have mercy on us.

STATION 13: JESUS IS TAKEN DOWN FROM THE CROSS

STATION 13

JESUS IS TAKEN DOWN FROM THE CROSS

V. We adore Thee, O Christ, and we bless Thee.

R. Because by Thy holy Cross, Thou hast redeemed the world.

Consider how, after the death of our Lord, two of His disciples, Joseph and Nicodemus, took Him down from the Cross, and placed Him in the arms of His afflicted Mother, who received Him with unutterable tenderness, and pressed Him to her bosom.

O Mother of sorrow, for the love of this Son, accept me for thy servant, and pray to Him for me. And Thou, my Redeemer, since Thou hast died for me, permit me to love Thee; for I wish but Thee, and nothing more. I love Thee, my Jesus, and I repent of ever having offended Thee. Never permit me to offend Thee again. Grant that I may love Thee always; and then do with me what Thou wilt.

Our Father, Hail Mary and Glory Be.

Dear Jesus, Thou dost go to die
For very love of me:
Ah! let me bear Thee company;
I wish to die with Thee.

V. Have mercy on us, O Lord.

R. Have mercy on us.

STATION 14: JESUS IS PLACED IN THE TOMB

STATION 14

JESUS IS PLACED IN THE TOMB

V. We adore Thee, O Christ, and we bless Thee.

R. Because by Thy holy Cross, Thou hast redeemed the world.

Consider how the disciples carried the body of Jesus to bury it, accompanied by His holy Mother, who arranged it in the sepulchre with her own hands. They then closed the tomb, and all withdrew.

Oh, my buried Jesus, I kiss the stone that encloses Thee. But Thou didst rise again the third day. I beseech Thee, by Thy resurrection, make me rise glorious with Thee at the last day, to be always united with Thee in heaven, to praise Thee and love Thee forever. I love Thee, and I repent of ever having offended Thee. Never permit me to offend Thee again. Grant that I may love Thee always; and then do with me what Thou wilt.

Our Father, Hail Mary and Glory Be.

Dear Jesus, Thou dost go to die
For very love of me:
Ah! let me bear Thee company;
I wish to die with Thee.

V. Have mercy on us, O Lord.

R. Have mercy on us.

ENDING

After this, say the Our Father, Hail Mary and Glory Be, five times, in honour of the Passion of Jesus Christ, to gain other indulgences granted those who recite them. Lastly, say one Our Father, Hail Mary and Glory Be, for the intention of the Sovereign Pontiff. Optional; Stabat Mater or Stabat Mater–Latin.

St Alphonsus Liguori, Pray for us! Amen.

PRAYERS

GLORY BE

Glory Be to the Father, and to the Son, and to the Holy Spirit. As it was in the beginning, is now, and ever shall be, world without end. Amen.

HAIL MARY

Hail Mary, Full of Grace, The Lord is with Thee. Blessed art Thou among women, and Blessed is the Fruit of Thy Womb, Jesus. Holy Mary, Mother of God, pray for us sinners now, and at the hour of death. Amen.

OUR FATHER

Our Father, Who art in Heaven, Hallowed be Thy Name. Thy Kingdom come, Thy Will be done, On earth as it is in Heaven. Give us this day Our daily bread, and Forgive us our trespasses as we forgive those who trespass against us. And lead us not into temptation, but deliver us from evil. Amen.

ACT OF CONTRITION

O my God, because You are so good. I am very sorry that I have sinned against You; and with the help of Your Grace, I will try not to sin again. Amen.

STABAT MATER

At the Cross her station keeping,
stood the mournful Mother weeping,
close to her Son to the last.
Through her heart, His sorrow sharing,
all His bitter anguish bearing,
now at length the sword has passed.

O how sad and sore distressed
was that Mother, highly blest,
of the sole-begotten One.

Christ above in torment hangs,
she beneath beholds the pangs
of her dying glorious Son.

Is there one who would not weep,
whelmed in miseries so deep,
Christ's dear Mother to behold?

Can the human heart refrain
from partaking in her pain,
in that Mother's pain untold?

For the sins of His own nation,
She saw Jesus wracked with torment,
All with scourges rent:

She beheld her tender Child,
Saw Him hang in desolation,
Till His spirit forth He sent.

O thou Mother! fount of love!
Touch my spirit from above,
make my heart with thine accord:

Make me feel as thou hast felt;
make my soul to glow and melt
with the love of Christ my Lord.

Holy Mother! pierce me through,
in my heart each wound renew
of my Savior crucified:

Let me share with thee His pain,
who for all my sins was slain,
who for me in torments died.

Let me mingle tears with thee,
mourning Him who mourned for me,
all the days that I may live:

By the Cross with thee to stay,
there with thee to weep and pray,
is all I ask of thee to give.

Virgin of all virgins blest!,
Listen to my fond request:
let me share thy grief divine;

Let me, to my latest breath,
in my body bear the death
of that dying Son of thine.

Wounded with His every wound,
steep my soul till it hath swooned,
in His very Blood away;

Be to me, O Virgin, nigh,
lest in flames I burn and die,
in His awful Judgment Day.

Christ, when Thou shalt call me hence,

by Thy Mother my defense,
by Thy Cross my victory;

While my body here decays,
may my soul Thy goodness praise,
Safe in Paradise with Thee.

STABAT MATER–LATIN

Stabat mater dolorosa
juxta Crucem lacrimosa,
dum pendebat Filius.

Cuius animam gementem,
contristatam et dolentem
pertransivit gladius.

O quam tristis et afflicta
fuit illa benedicta,
mater Unigeniti!

Quae moerebat et dolebat,
pia Mater, dum videbat
nati poenas inclyti.

Quis est homo qui non fleret,
matrem Christi si videret
in tanto supplicio?

Quis non posset contristari
Christi Matrem contemplari
dolentem cum Filio?

Pro peccatis suae gentis
vidit Iesum in tormentis,
et flagellis subditum.

Vidit suum dulcem Natum
moriendo desolatum,
dum emisit spiritum.

Eia, Mater, fons amoris
me sentire vim doloris
fac, ut tecum lugeam.

Fac, ut ardeat cor meum
in amando Christum Deum
ut sibi complaceam.

Sancta Mater, istud agas,
crucifixi fige plagas
cordi meo valide.

Tui Nati vulnerati,
tam dignati pro me pati,
poenas mecum divide.

Fac me tecum pie flere,
crucifixo condolere,
donec ego vixero.

Juxta Crucem tecum stare,
et me tibi sociare
in planctu desidero.

Virgo virginum praeclara,
mihi iam non sis amara,
fac me tecum plangere.

Fac, ut portem Christi mortem,
passionis fac consortem,
et plagas recolere.

Fac me plagis vulnerari,

fac me Cruce inebriari,
et cruore Filii.

Flammis ne urar succensus,
per te, Virgo, sim defensus
in die iudicii.

Christe, cum sit hinc exire,
da per Matrem me venire
ad palmam victoriae.

Quando corpus morietur,
fac, ut animae donetur
paradisi gloria. Amen.

CATHOLIC WAY PUBLISHING

QUALITY PAPERBACKS AND E-BOOKS

TRUE DEVOTION TO MARY: WITH PREPARATION FOR TOTAL CONSECRATION
BY SAINT LOUIS DE MONTFORT

6" x 9" Hardback: ISBN–13: 978-1-78379-004-3
6" x 9" Paperback: ISBN–13: 978-1-78379-011-1
5" x 8" Paperback: ISBN–13: 978-1-78379-000-5
MOBI E-Book: ISBN–13: 978-1-78379-001-2
EPUB E-Book: ISBN–13: 978-1-78379-002-9

THE SECRET OF THE ROSARY BY SAINT LOUIS DE MONTFORT

5" x 8" Paperback: ISBN–13: 978-1-78379-310-5
MOBI E-Book: ISBN–13: 978-1-78379-311-2
EPUB E-Book: ISBN–13: 978-1-78379-312-9

THE IMITATION OF CHRIST BY THOMAS A KEMPIS

5" x 8" Paperback: ISBN–13: 978-1-78379-037-1
MOBI E-Book: ISBN–13: 978-1-78379-038-8
EPUB E-Book: ISBN–13: 978-1-78379-039-5

MY DAILY PRAYERS BY CATHOLIC WAY PUBLISHING

5" x 8" Paperback: ISBN–13: 978-1-78379-027-2
MOBI E-Book: ISBN–13: 978-1-78379-028-9
EPUB E-Book: ISBN–13: 978-1-78379-029-6

THE MYSTICAL CITY OF GOD: POPULAR ABRIDGEMENT
BY VENERABLE MARY OF AGREDA

5" x 8" Paperback: ISBN–13: 978-1-78379-063-0
MOBI E-Book: ISBN–13: 978-1-78379-064-7
EPUB E-Book: ISBN–13: 978-1-78379-065-4

THE THREE AGES OF THE INTERIOR LIFE: PRELUDE OF ETERNAL LIFE
BY REVEREND REGINALD GARRIGOU-LAGRANGE O.P.

5" x 8" Paperback Volume 1: ISBN–13: 978-1-78379-405-8
5" x 8" Paperback Volume 2: ISBN–13: 978-1-78379-406-5
MOBI E-Book: ISBN–13: 978-1-78379-407-2
EPUB E-Book: ISBN–13: 978-1-78379-408-9

CATHOLIC WAY PUBLISHING

www.catholicwaypublishing.com
London, England, UK
2015

14472906R00044

Printed in Great Britain
by Amazon.co.uk, Ltd.,
Marston Gate.